Goods:
From Here to There

CONTENTS

NATIONAL GEOGRAPHIC   Hampton-Brown

School Publishing

Words with **ch**, **tch**

Look at each picture. Read the words.

ch
_tch

Example:

check

pi**tch**

chips

chick

ran**ch**

scra**tch**

High Frequency
Words

| around |
| be |
| here |
| need |
| together |
| where |

Key Words

Look at the picture.
Read the sentences.

Chicks and More Chicks

1. The chicks like to **be together**.
2. They hop **around** the hen.
3. They **need** to eat. **Where** can they eat?
4. The chicks find bugs **here** in the grass.

What do the chicks eat?

GO! **Phonics Games**
NGReach.com

3

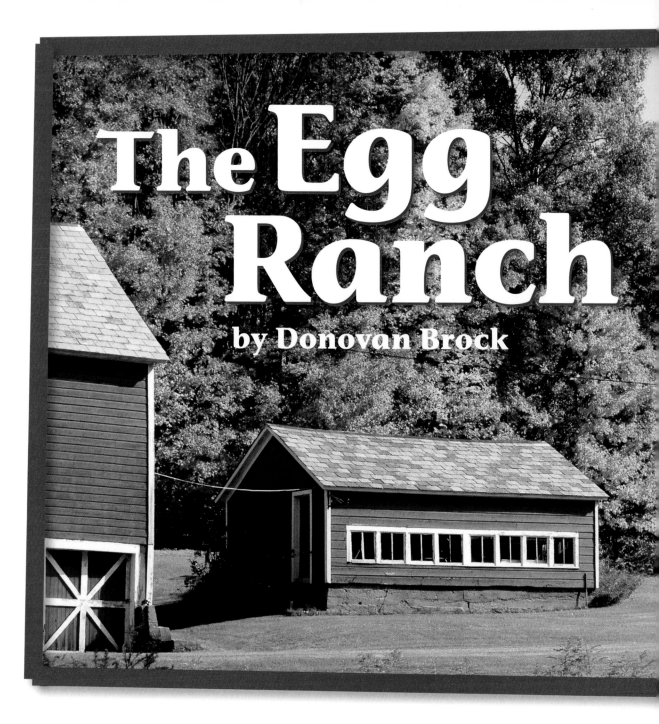

The Egg Ranch

by Donovan Brock

This is an egg ranch. How does it work?

It starts with hens. Hens lay
the eggs.

Eggs hatch at the ranch. The chicks will grow up here.

food

Scratch, scratch, scratch! The chicks
scratch around together for food. Peck,
peck, peck! The hens chomp on bugs.

hutch

nest

The chicks live in a hutch, but the hens need nests.

The hens lay such a big batch of eggs! The eggs need to be kept chilled.

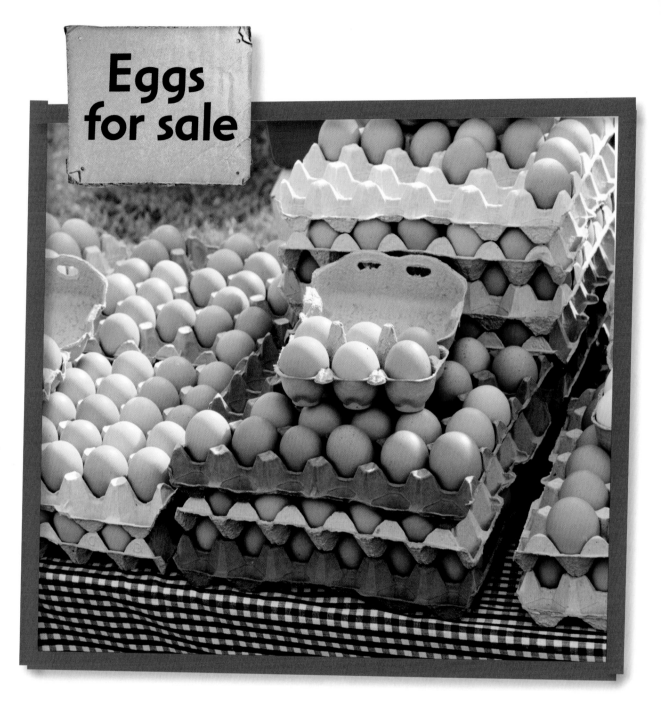

Eggs for sale

You can get eggs at a stand like this or in the store. Where do you get your eggs? ❖

Words with ch, tch

Read these words.

chick	chop	dog	fetch
hen	man	ranch	scratch

Find the words with **ch** and **tch**. Use letters to build them.

r   a   n   c   h

Talk Together

Tell your partner what you can see at the egg ranch. Use words from the box above.

I can see a chick scratch.

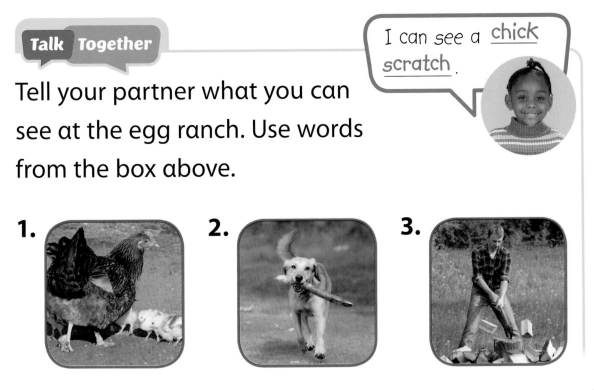

1. 2. 3.

11

Words with th

Look at the pictures. Read the words.

th

Example:

ba**th**

thick

thin

pa**th**

clo**th**

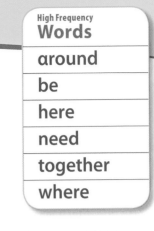

High Frequency
Words

around
be
here
need
together
where

Key Words

Look at the pictures.
Read the sentences.

Find Good Food

1. **Where** can we buy good food? Dad said we do not **need** to go to the big store.
2. We went **together** to the farm stand.
3. Dad asked for things that grow **around** **here**.
4. He said they will **be** fresh and cost less.

What would you get?

Phonics Games
NGReach.com

13

The Cost of Things

by Deanne W. Kells

$300.00

The cloth in this quilt is
stitched together by hand.

machine

$40.00

A machine stitched together the cloth in this quilt.

The quilt stitched by hand costs more. Why?

$50.00

This dog bed is thick.

$15.00

This dog bed is thin. Does the
thick bed cost more or less?

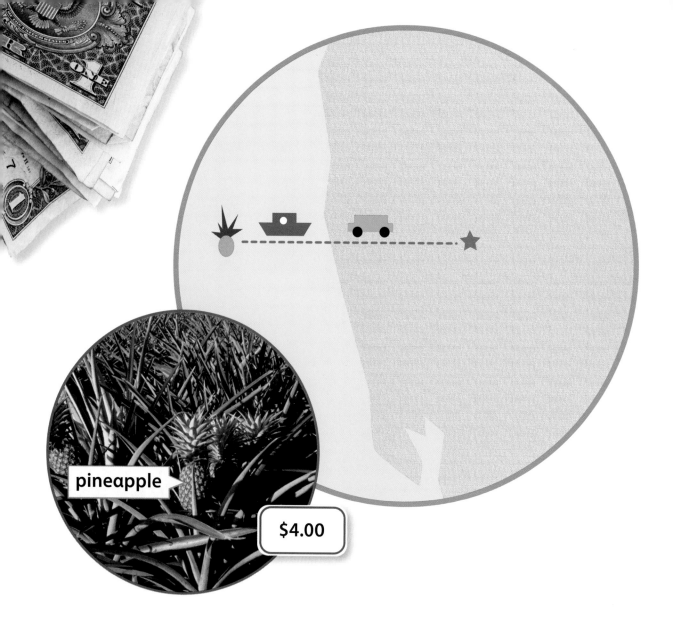

pineapple

$4.00

Pineapples can not grow where
I live. They are sent here on a ship
and then on a truck.

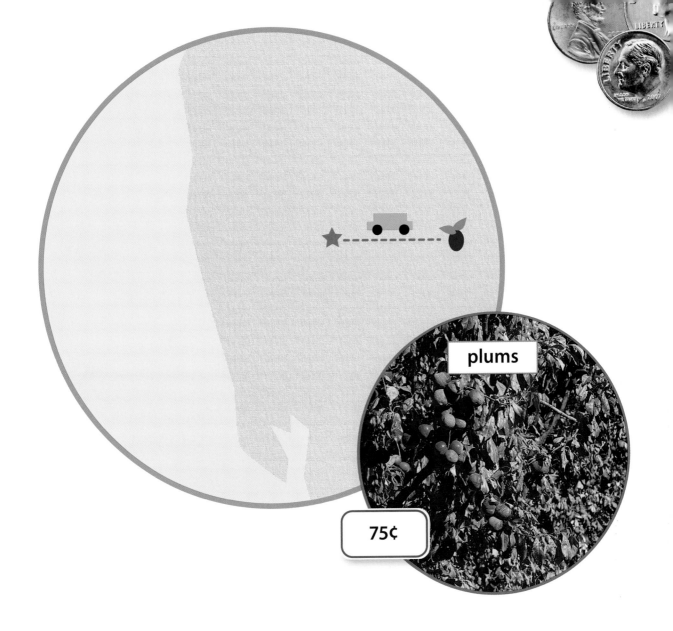

plums

75¢

Plums can grow on the land
around here. They are sent on a truck.
Why do the plums cost less?

Do you see why things cost more?

Think of this: How is it put together?

Where is it from? ❖

Words with <u>th</u>

Read these words.

bath	cloth	grass	pink
red	thank	thick	thin

Find the words with **-th**. Use letters to build the words.

b | a | t | h

Talk Together

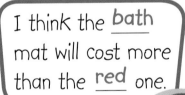

I think the <u>bath</u> mat will cost more than the <u>red</u> one.

Choose words from the box above to tell your partner about the costs of the mats.

Grass Mats

Mat Shop

Cloth Mats

Bath Mats

Back to the Ranch

Cowgirl Jan must get back to the ranch!
Help her stay on the right path. Trace
the path with your finger.

1. First, go over the ditch, not around it.
2. Next, pass by a thick tree and a thin tree growing together.
3. Now you need to be on the path with the red cloth flag.
4. Finally, go to where the cow chomps on grass.
5. You are here at the ranch!

Acknowledgments

Grateful acknowledgment is given to the authors, artists, photographers, museums, publishers, and agents for permission to reprint copyrighted material. Every effort has been made to secure the appropriate permission. If any omissions have been made or if corrections are required, please contact the Publisher.

Photographic Credits

CVR (br) erwo1/iStockphoto. (tl) DAJ/Getty Images. **2** (bl) Danita Delimont/Alamy Images. (br) Juniors Bildarchiv/Alamy Images. (cl) redmal/iStockphoto. (cr) Karen Roach/Shutterstock. (tr) DigitalStock/Corbis. **3** (b) Liz Garza Williams/Hampton-Brown/National Geographic School Publishing. (t) Poznukhov Yuriy/Shutterstock. **4** Don Blais/Shutterstock. **5** Juniors Bildarchiv/ Alamy Images. **6** David Aubrey/Photo Researchers, Inc.. **7** Wildlife/Peter Arnold, Inc.. **8** (b) Peter Anderson/Getty Images. (t) Becky McCray. **9** Chris Windsor/Getty Images. (inset) Jochen Arndt/Getty Images. **10** (b) Gordon Dixon/iStockphoto. (t) magicinfoto/Shutterstock. **11** (bc) Jean Frooms/Shutterstock. (br) Wiktor Bubniak/iStockphoto. (lc) Four Oaks/Shutterstock. (t) Liz Garza Williams/Hampton-Brown/National Geographic School Publishing. **12** (bl) Littleman/Shutterstock. (br) Arcoindex/Shutterstock. (tl) Gelpi/Shutterstock. (tr) Antonov Roman/Shutterstock. **13** (b) Liz Garza Williams/Hampton-Brown/National Geographic School Publishing. (tl) MBI/Alamy Images. (tr) Krisztina Farkas/Shutterstock. **14** (b) Keith Webber Jr./ iStockphoto. (t) karen roach/Shutterstock. **15** (b) Cappi Thompson/Shutterstock. (t) Sergey Goruppa/Alamy Images. **16** Tom Nance/Shutterstock. **17** (c) Elliot Westacott/Shutterstock. (t) Cappi Thompson/Shutterstock. **18** (bl) Peter and Georgina Bowater/Tips Italia/Photolibrary. (t) karen roach/Shutterstock. **19** (br) Chris L Jones/Photolibrary. (t) Cappi Thompson/ Shutterstock. **20** (bl) Dan Barnes/iStockphoto. (br) iofoto/Shutterstock. (tl) Keith Webber Jr./ iStockphoto. (tr) Sergey Goruppa/Alamy Images. **21** (t) Liz Garza Williams/Hampton-Brown/ National Geographic School Publishing.

Illustrator Credits

21, 22-23 Peter Grosshauer

The National Geographic Society

John M. Fahey, Jr., President & Chief Executive Officer
Gilbert M. Grosvenor, Chairman of the Board

National Geographic School Publishing
Hampton-Brown
www.NGSP.com

Printed in the USA.
RR Donnelley, Jefferson City, MO

ISBN:978-0-7362-8032-7

12 13 14 15 16 17 18 19
10 9 8 7 6 5 4